MY STORY, GOD'S GLORY

SECOND EDITION

By Rev. Dr. Margaret Smith

My Story, God's Glory
Second Edition
By Rev. Dr. Margaret Smith

Copyright ©2019
By Rev. Dr. Margaret Smith

Layout by Rev. Dr. Margaret Smith

Published By: Rev Dr. Margaret Smith
www.impactcovenantministries.org

Rev. Dr. Margaret Smith, Author & Publisher
Printed in the United States of America

Second Edition December 2019

TABLE OF CONTENTS

Chapter 1

Faith Journey in Ministry

In the first edition of "My Story, God's Glory", I shared a summarized version of my personal and ministerial journey as the Holy Spirit inspired me to write.

If you did not purchase a copy for your library, let me give you a brief update. I shared my experiences growing up in a single-parent home, my educational development, and career path. Also, ministry in my country Jamaica - relocation and continuation of my ministry including obstacles, my son's legal battle, and more. Also praise reports of God's divine interventions. I also took you on some side excursions magnifying the fact that God is not a figment of our imagination but is very real. So, I pray that you will get a hold of my first edition and be blessed by its inspirational and empowering words.

As I continue on this wonderful journey, my focus is on ministry, but I will also include a synopsis of my son's journey with a legal battle.

I have learned so much about people as I journeyed alongside them. I believe all of us suffers from some amount of insecurity. It could be because of limited achievements, negative words spoken over our lives or just plain walking in our human condition, which sometimes, gives room to jealousy.

I experienced struggles with insecurities also. This has been due, mostly, to negative and nonproductive associations. People with habitual negative thinking and speaking, as well as being disrespectful to me or in my presence. These types of behavior made me feel very uncomfortable.

There were others who, as soon as they get comfortable in association, they think that they can cross established boundaries of familiarity, especially in professional environments. In other words, they disregard set boundaries. When their unacceptable behavior is reprimanded, they took offense displayed by body language that responds, "who do you think you are?" This became very disturbing and unacceptable to me. Therefore, I issued "time out" of tolerating these kinds of disrespectful behaviors.

I maintained this disposition, which will continue for the remainder of my days. I will prayerfully select people for my inner circle. Let me make this clear, we are to love everyone, especially in the Body of Christ. However, wisdom is important when choosing our inner circle. We should avoid making ourselves vulnerable to everyone.

Another unpleasant concern I had, was the fact that I love to acquire knowledge in various areas of interest. For example, the medical and mental health fields, and study of the Bible including tools that supplement various aspect of it, cultures, background, etc.

When I engage in discussions on these topics, there are those who tend to dominate the discussion. They want to magnify how knowledgeable they are, to the extent of not giving others, including myself, a word in edgewise. Sometimes, I can squeeze in my views. After or during the dialogue, I would sometimes be told, "You think you know it all" or "You come across as a know it all." That response would, sometimes, leave a bad taste in my mouth. However, now, I put it into perspective by saying, "Well, everyone has a right to express their opinion."

I have no control over what others think or say. So if I have something noteworthy when participating in a dialogue, I will say it, because it is my democratic right to do so.

Now let me be quick to say this, "first, I am a Christian Counselor by academics and anointing and a Teacher according to the five-fold ministry gifts. Therefore, sometime these giftings are reflected in my conversation and I sometimes, have the tendency to probe unnecessarily and respond to things that, in my opinion, were not required by others." Therefore, upon self-examination and the Holy Spirit's guidance, I have greatly improved on this flaw.

The Scripture says in Proverbs that we are ensnared by the words of our mouth. Also, even a fool when he keeps silent is thought of as being wise. So, I have, and continue to train myself to speak less and listen more. One thing I must say, is, I have a few close friends who, when I am in their presence, I can be free to express myself, even if it comes out ridiculous. Thank God for putting them in my   life.

So the point of this story is that we need to express the love of God to each other. God's love is not jealous, it is not proud, it is not rude, and it does not keep records of wrong, etc. 1Corinthians 13:1-8. I pray that Christians will allow the Holy Spirit to work in the flawed, carnal   areas   of   their   lives.

Another disturbing observation I had on this journey concerning dialogue with fellow Christians, is the issue of confidentiality.

Here is an example; my son, as indicated in the first edition of this publication, was faced with a legal battle. At first, I mentioned it to a few folks only as a legal battle; because no matter what public records reveal, a person is innocent until proven guilty. Also, since it was still in the courts and lawyers were assigned to the case, I knew it was important that very little information was released publicly. The law states, "Anything you say can be used against you in a court of law." Therefore, I shared very little details with a few persons, for prayer purposes only. But before I could count 1-2-3, it spread like wildfire. Some of the perpetrators are not aware that I know they shared information that I communicated to them in confidence. But I lift my eyes to God who knows all things.

These kind of behavior does not express the love of God. When someone confides in us, especially as believers, they do not expect us to share it with best friends, significant others, or anyone else. It is meant to be kept in confidence.

Here is the deal, your friend has their friends; your mate has their friends. Though it is very difficult not to pass on information, this is what confidentiality requires. I will be quick to say that God has given me some awesome friends and colleagues who stood with me in prayer and supported me in strict confidence. In other words, they had my back. Many thanks to all of you.

Many years ago, I worked at a banking institution in our Island and we had to sign a confidentiality document. Though this was about 30 years ago, I still maintain it to this day. Also, I have had friends that are related, but one never knew what the other shared with me, because it was not either of their concerns. So, this discipline is very sensitive to me and when violated can really hurt, but thank God for the gift of forgiveness.

I have learned and decided in the future that whoever I take into my confidence, must earn my vulnerability first. Now this should not have to be this way, because the Bible taught us to confess our faults one to the other and pray one for the other that we might be healed.

We should be able to share with each other, though wisdom suggest that we weigh the issues in the balance, by seeking the Holy Spirit before we make that critical decision of sharing it with others.

Here is an example that I shared for training purposes, with members of my team regarding confidentiality. If someone visits my home or office, having shared some very sensitive and private information with me, then immediately after they left, another mutual friend visits. I then mention that they visited to our mutual friend. Sometime afterwards, they both connected and friend "B" mentioned that I told her/him of their visit with me. Immediately friend "A" will start to wonder, how much of our confidential conversation was shared with friend "B". Therefore, to avoid mistrust, I reframe from sharing even that simple, but very sensitive piece of information regarding the visitation of our mutual friends to my office. This can cause trust issues. It is often said of me that I am too private, but I would rather that said of me, than that I am not   confidential.

Confidentiality is very important to me. I have had people volunteered info to me that I have had to say to them TMI - too much information. I did not need to know all that.

Also, we must always be careful of what we say among strangers, because we do not know "who knows who." So, in a public environment -restaurant, church group, even prayer request, we must use wisdom.

Some time ago I was with a friend, while one of her friends was transporting us. Her friend: the driver of the vehicle, answered a call via her car Bluetooth. She was speaking with someone that I did not know. However, during their conversation the person on the other end of the phone call started divulging sensitive information to the driver about someone I knew. My eyes popped, but I said nothing. It was that easy for sensitive information to be circulated because I could have shared that information back to my friend, but I did not. I probably would if it were necessary. So, the learning experience that I want to communicate is this; if someone did not give you any message to share, do not!

The Bible says, "They will know we are Christians by our love." So those of you who shared sensitive information re my son's legal battle, I am disappointed, but I forgive you.

Another crushing thing regarding my son's situation was, persons who my son did so much for both young and old, who were like family to him, turned their backs on him during his season of trials and tribulation. "But God".

As we continue to journey through this season of discomfort, Jeremiah 29:11 declares, "for I know the plans I have for you, plans that are good and not evil to give you hope and a future." He is coming out like Joseph from the pit to the palace. As I am writing, this is at the dawning of the day in his life altering experiences. God is constantly with him and has worked everything out for his good. Hallelujah!!

JOURNAL

Use this page to write your experiences with God as you go through the chapters of the journey with me.

Chapter 2

Full-time   Ministry   Experiences

As I continue this journey, walking by faith, God showed Himself strong on my behalf. I am thankful that God gave to me a faithful group of people who continues to support me while being on the frontline of ministry, serving through thick and thin. Some went on to launch their own ministries based on principles and truths imparted in our training and empowerment programs. Others departed for various other reasons in which case I gave my blessings, though I was somewhat disappointed with some of their timing and departure. However, I am confident that all things work together for good. Some have expressed renewed respect for me because they are now realizing what it takes to grow a ministry.

One thing I observed about some of these individuals that served alongside me, is the fact that some found it difficult to take the leap and launch out from their comfort zone. Some pretended to follow instructions but secretly complained during the process. As a seasoned leader, I understood these immature behaviors and emotional struggles.

There are many Mentees that the Lord allowed me to guide to their purpose/assignment. Unfortunately, some were influenced by the spirit of jealousy and ego. It caused them to become deceptive in their communication to friends and connections. They communicated negative things just to magnify themselves. I realize, now, that all or most of the people they previously complained about, resulted from their deceptive nature. But I continue to pray God's deliverance for them; It is a process that only God can prepare us for, as leaders.

One major challenge I have had over the years is appointing someone to take over when I transition. I believe God has selected some and brought them to my ministry, but because of fear of failure, they bend and succumbed to their inabilities to maintain consistency in the spirit of excellence and professionalism.

The mentality of most legalistic Christians is to say "Let the spirit have His way" while they behave out of order, and for them anything goes. But the truth is, if the Holy Spirit were having His way then His character would be reflected. The Bible says, God is not the author of confusion; therefore, everything must be in order according to His Word.

I am still praying and trusting God that my support base will remain consistent as Aaron and Hurr in holding up my arms, and my Joshua to carry-on the battle for the manifestation of the vision. He who began a good work shall perform it to the end.

Someone shared a story recently which is such a great example of being on a journey and the process and challenges it takes to arrive at the designated destination;

"It was January 24, 1848 when James W. Marshall discovered a gold nugget in the American River, while constructing a sawmill for John Sutter, a Sacramento agriculturalists." This period was referred to as "The Gold Rush in California."

"The news spread like wildfire throughout regions. The gold rush conjured up story images of thousands of "49" heading west in wagons to strike it rich in California, but many actually arrived by ship."

The story to illustrate my point came from those images. So, there were some cowboys and their families, as they were called back in the day. They ventured out to get a piece of the action. They gathered a "posse" traveling in wagons, today known as a convoy," of other interested families to go with them. However, while on the journey, they had to make a few rests stops in different regions. During some of the stops they encountered many dangers due to bandits/robbers, etc.

Eventually, some of the travelers decided they had as much as they could take, so they decided to end their journey where they stopped, while others returned home. However, the leader was determined to get to the destination, so he and his family continued. They refused to allow anyone or any circumstances to stop them. They finally arrived at their destination in California, which was victorious for them. The point of this story is that, though some followers, etc., may fall by the wayside on the designated journey. As Leaders, we should not allow these distractions to destroy us; we must keep moving forward. The Bible instructs us to move   forward.

Many obstacles came my way, including divorce, financial issues, transportation, legal issues with son, deception in relationships, you name it, I have experienced it. But I must say, "There has been many victories" – miracles, sign, and wonders truly follows those that believe God.

JOURNAL

Use this page to write your experiences with God as you go through the chapters of the journey with me.

Chapter 3

Leading While Bleeding

This title means that, as I went through tough situations, regardless of how painful they were, I continued serving in my ministerial leadership responsibilities and activities.

Throughout these times, I have proven that God is truly the strength of my life. Some people focus only on the importance of their needs and believe that Ministers are called to serve regardless of their own circumstances. Though they are aware of some of the hardships Ministers go through, most do not put it into proper perspective. So, to protect myself from being overwhelmed, I do my best to maintain clear boundaries, regarding my schedule.

However, in their defense, sometimes it is not that they are inconsiderate, but the perception of a Leader/Minister is that they are super humans, designed to function in their positions, regardless of their own pain and fatigue.

Let me pause here to speak to Ministers, Pastors, and other Leaders. Please carve out time to refresh yourselves. Take vacations, go on sabbaticals, spend quality "me-times", and include God. Jesus led by example when He would often leave His disciples and went off into the mountain by Himself to pray and to be restored. God revealed this to us in the beginning by resting on the seventh day.

The nature of the job is highly stress related. Someone once said, "Our bodies are very intelligent, and if we don't follow the signs it gives us regarding when to stop, then it will stop us."

People are always going to need help, but we are not designed to save the entire world on our own. Each joint supply. God has assigned us our customized group of people to minister to. It took me some time to acknowledge this fact. However, I do know when to say no to invitations that I am unable to accept, due to my God ordained assignment.

Here is the other part of my pause; there is a mindset by some ministries that if you do not support them, they will not support your program. I strongly believe that this type of behavior has wrong motives and is a type of manipulation.

If an organization or person cannot support your event, you should still support theirs, if possible. Even if they do not return the favor. Let the love of God lead you.

Jesus gave of Himself knowing that we would never be able to repay Him. The love of God is unconditional. This behavior of trying to be everywhere because you want your event to be supported, is not Godly. Therefore, let us be wise and allow God to be our guide; end pause.

Though I was bleeding, figuratively speaking,

for over four and a half years because of my challenging experiences. I continued with the help of God on the journey to fulfilling His call on my life. It was also financially draining. However, God made ways for us out of what seem to have been no way. During this season of bleeding while leading, lives were being tremendously impacted by the Lord through me, and my ministry Team.

I learned a lot during these tough times. One is, when you work hard with God's help in accomplishing your goals, there will be people around you who are genuinely happy for you, while others will be overtaken with jealousy.

During these times, there were folks who misguidedly perceived that our ministry was experiencing great financial increase due to our external appearance. So, a couple partners discontinued their financial support abruptly. This type of reaction was out of ignorance and lack of commitment to God.

There was also a phase in my ministry, especially, during the time when my books were being published. The impression for some donors was that we were now financially stable and no longer needed their financial resources.

Another challenge was being without transportation for a couple years, until God finally made a way out of no way and provided reliable transportation. Again, a few covenant partners paused their contributions. Others severely decreased their financial support. The ministry's financial position almost screeched to a halt – the bare minimum came in. But God! This action came during a very challenging crisis.

However, God kept opened new doors and for that I am very grateful. I am talking about leading while bleeding. Though these challenges made my heart bleed, I continued to be the Leader God called me to be. It is His strength in me that kept me going. God is truly the strength of my life.

I encourage all Ministers and Leaders. Do not become weary in well doing, because your reward shall be great. Even if there were not going to be additional rewards. What Jesus did for us is more than enough. So, hold on, be strong and courageous. It will be worth it all.

Keep your eyes on Jesus. Paul, the Apostle, continued to minister, although he bled (endured hardship) from a prison cell. I leave you with this analogy; "If we are to enjoy the awesome, tasty juices from grapes, they have to be crushed." Therefore, hardship ultimately will produce great rewards.

I pause again to look at my accomplishments. I have to acknowledge that I cannot take all the credit, because with everything I had to deal with and still achieve my goals, it had to be the strength and energy of God that helped me accomplish them.

I am also grateful to some awesome sisters(spiritual), colleagues and friends, who never gave up on me. They stood with me, giving their time and financial support. I thank God also for my family, especially my son, who is my motivation to keep going.

I thank God for inspiring Sarah Young, a woman of God who I hope to meet some day. She inspired and motivated me through her devotional book, 'Jesus Calling.' God truly knows how to put people in our lives, both negative and positive, because whether we believe it or not, they both play significant roles.

Also, during those hard times, our ministry, target audience were being blessed and delivered through our programs, especially our counseling, events, and community benevolence outreach services. 98% of marital issues have been resolved; pre-marital sessions helped with Godly decision-making process. Youth personal development programs assisted many young people in making good choices. Some strayed but are learning from their mistakes.

Our Intercessory prayer ministry reached the sick, financially challenged, resolved immigration issues. Women of all ages and families are empowered through our training program of building strong self-esteem and self-confidence.

It is tough to lead while bleeding, but God promised that He will be with us through the fire and the floods and nothing shall by any means harm us. This kind of bleeding is not to destroy us but to strengthen us.

The Apostle Paul said it best:
"Therefore, to keep me from becoming conceited, I was given a thorn in the flesh, a messenger of Satan, to torment me. Three times I pleaded with the Lord to take it away from me. But He said to me, "My grace is sufficient for you, for my power is made perfect in weakness. "Therefore, I will boast all the more gladly about my weaknesses, so that Christ's power may rest on me."

Through all the pain and challenges, my ministry, Impact, is positioned for greatness. We are trusting God to release the ultimate source of finance.

While on this part of the journey – Leading while Bleeding, I encountered various Ministry Leaders and Colleagues who, unknowingly, taught me many things. One of which is; We are all flawed vessels and need to be careful how vulnerable we allow ourselves to be with others in the faith, because some are still struggling with weaknesses including gossip, jealousy, insecurities, deception and numerous others.

I recently read a post on a popular social media. The individual was very descriptive of how well she played church and ministry. Having gone to high levels of service, but she was still not delivered from the bondage of serving with wrong motives - Talking the talk but not walking the walk.

She confessed openly her bondage of deception and her deliverance. She posted her testimony in order to bring awareness and to confirm that only God can effect change in a person's life, as they yield to Him. Without God, our abilities are ineffective.

When you study the lives of our forefathers and Jesus' disciples, you will observe that when the Holy Spirit visited or came upon them, their lives were transformed. We are in a fallen world; therefore, it is possible to operate with evil tendencies. However, through Jesus Christ we were regenerated.

The song says, "The same power that raised Jesus from the dead is in us." So, all we have to do is to yield to the Holy Spirit's control.

Join me in a prayer of repentance for the many times we took over the role of the Holy Spirit, trying to change ourselves and others.

Prayer
"Lord, please forgive us for trying to take over the role of the Holy Spirit in our lives and the lives of others. We give that back to you. We surrender the responsibility of change to you in Jesus' name." Amen.

Another experience of my bleeding while leading involved my accommodations. I gave up my comfortable place of residence as indicated in my first book. This was a challenge, because I have never been involved in roommate type experience, but I did what I was led to do at the time. Wow!

I had many experiences in the few homes I stayed. However, I am grateful to God, now for them, but when I was in it, because it was very new to me, it was very difficult. I give God thanks that the majority of those who hosted me were amazing. I honor everyone who were so gracious to me with their hospitality.

Eventually I was restored to a comfortable space, so I got my chance to "give forward" by assisting those who were transitioning and needed temporary space until they "got back on their feet." I desired to be a blessing considering my past situation. I knew that I did not want these individuals to feel uncomfortable as they go through their temporary displacement. So the few cases I assisted, I went the extra mile in being accommodating so that these persons would experience the love of Jesus.

I thank God for the obedience of those who open their doors to me and gave me a place to rest on this awesome journey!! Even a cup of water given to a prophet of God reaps great rewards. These were truly times of bleeding.

I am also mindful and impress on others to be mindful of the scripture that says, "Be careful how you entertain strangers, as you could be entertaining Angels, unawares." The first thing Abraham did when he saw the two strangers coming to his house, was to respectfully receive them, because he perceived something was different about them. He immediately requested the best food to be prepared and presented to them.

Note also, the prophet Elijah and the family who provided a home for him to rest. In some of my experiences I noted that some took for granted the anointing on my life-familiarity syndrome. But that's ok because God had it under His control.

Then I also remembered Jesus' experience with his own family and friends, they saw him as just their brother, friend, son etc., and because of that, he could only do very little miracles among them. He said, I could perform very little miracles because of familiarity.

Let me pause here to remind us that God placed rich deposits in us before we entered the earth realm. How do I know this? He said to Jeremiah, "before you were formed in your mother's womb, I ordained you to be a Prophet." Therefore, we need to respect each other's anointing.

God gave gifts to us for the edification of the body of Christ, not to brag or to think of ourselves higher than each other. We need each other's anointing to complete the assignment we have been given by God.

What I have observed among us, as believers, is that the environment influences us in our human development and causes us to develop negative habits. Things such as insecurities, identity crisis, low self-esteem, and self-confidence issues, influenced us to strive for positions of power that we, sometimes, lose focus of our God ordained purpose - ultimately praise to God.

In the prayer, Jesus taught us, He said, "Thine is the kingdom, the power and the glory, forever." So, we need to humble ourselves and treat everyone with respect and honor. It should not matter what is your socioeconomic and educational status. Anybody can achieve any status if they put their mind to it. So, none of us have any bragging rights. It is God who gives, and he can take away.

My prayer is that, at this juncture, we will allow the Holy Spirit to mold and make us until we are restored to the likeness and image of God. People need the Lord - not our might or power. We are to be the hands and feet of

God, operational in the earth.

It makes me very sad to see, as Christians, how we treat each other. But I am here to bring Hope. So, I challenge us today that we go out of our way to be kind to everyone we meet. This will leave an indelible mark upon their lives.

Maya Angelo said, "People will forget what you say or do to them but will never forget how you make them feel."

There might not be any special awards here on the earth, but there is someone that is taking notes. The Bible states that there is a day of reckoning coming. The Bible also declares; Jesus speaking, "when I was hungry you never fed me, when I was in prison you never visited me..."

Jesus also said, "Whatever you did to the least of these, you did it unto me." So we should work towards hearing "well done", instead of "depart from me, I know you not".

It was not easy for me to digest, as I was at the receiving end of some who pride themselves on being powerhouse Christians, yet treat fellow believers with such disrespect. It is indescribable to mention. These same people would go and preach or teach some of the best sermons. 1Corinthians 13:1-8 should be their anthem. All these experiences constituted bleeding while leading.

Another bleeding experience I encountered was Jealousy, especially among females. Some found it very difficult to celebrate others whom God has placed in their lives. Especially those with material success. Honor is being replaced with slander and gossip. We should be comfortable in celebrating what God has done for others among the family of God, understanding that our breakthrough will come, and we will need someone to celebrate us.

So, as I previously referenced my personal achievement. I can truly say God deserves all the glory. God opened and shut doors and removed people from my inner circle; repositioned me in places where I gained divine connections and favor.

There were times when I thought some of the favors I had, were naturally what others of like faith experienced. But as I compared notes, I realized that it was God's divine intervention. Therefore, throughout my period of leading while bleeding, I learned from all my encounters. In other words, all things work together in harmony for our good and God's glory.

JOURNAL

Use this page to write your experiences with God as you go through the chapters of the journey with me.

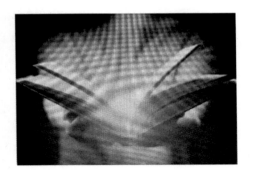

Chapter 4

Isolation

During school, a student had to be tested to prove their knowledge in a subject. So, it is in our Journey from glory to glory. There are various levels of testing. It is in those times of testing; God seem to be quiet.

A few years ago, I volunteered to serve as a proctor during school state examination. Proctors are placed in the room to guide and answer questions unrelated to the answers to the test. Anything else is against the rules and has penalties.

Due to the fact that I am functioning full-time in Ministry, my type of testing is trusting God to provide my daily needs in order to keep the ministry active.

One of my personal challenge and discomfort is asking for donation, when people lack knowledge regarding the topic of sowing into ministry, according to God's Word. Some people can be very insensitive, because they do not acknowledge it as investment in Kingdom projects.

Therefore, I did not want to experience this, but as I meditated on scriptures such as Proverb 3, Psalm 24, Psalm 23, they constantly reminded me that God owns everything and when we trust Him, He will direct our path; pathways to people and entities that are obedient in releasing the resources needed for Kingdom building.

The devil focus his attack in this area to try to block God's provision, but I declare that, "no weapon formed against me shall prosper and greater is he that is in me than he that is in the world."

Also, constant prayer, praise and thanksgiving to God causes vengeance to be executed upon our enemies, psalm 149. Many times, the testing seem so tough. I almost let go, but when I remembered how Jesus stuck it out all the way to Calvary, just to pay the price for our freedom, I held on to His unchanging hand.

Paul is also a point of reference for me as seen in Scriptures. He endured so much to finish the assignment God called him to do.

Based on this chapter title, a major test I faced was isolation. Sometimes I would be looking to hear from my friends and colleagues, even family members, but very little contacts. However, I gave God thanks for few consistent contacts from my Team and a very extraordinary close friend who remain consistent in my life.

When I experience loneliness - needing someone to just share my inner thoughts, this person, who God gave to me as a confidant is always there for me. Thank you Jesus, please pour out blessings upon this person. Amen!!

Sometimes the enemy would send thoughts such as you are not needed by anyone. I looked at him under my feet and say, "Devil, you are a liar." I realized it was God testing me. During these times of isolation, He gave me instructions regarding His assignments.

During those times, I also thought of how God allowed the children of Israel to rest in Him. He would not allow the cloud or the pillar of fire to move for days. This would give them time to learn to rest and refuel for the rest of the journey.

Pausing and resting is not easy, because the world system taught us to always be busy or we will not accomplish our goals within a given timeline. But a thousand years with God is like a day. So, God already has a perfect plan for our lives, Jeremiah 29:11.

So I struggled with these seemingly downtimes, but the Holy Spirit helped and continues to help me through. My tendency is to try to help God in pushing things faster through my times of isolation. Also, the Holy Spirit gave me the strength to resist the temptation of trying to help God.

There were times, also that the devil uses even the closest people to me to suggest great ideas of things I needed to do, especially in areas of income. The Bible says, "Those who know their God are strong and can-do mighty exploits."

In my experience, I have found that these

were the times when God revealed Himself to me in an awesome way and speak to the hearts of others to provide the needed resources for ministry. This might not be your experience, because God deals with us in different ways, according to His purpose for our lives.

Example, Peter and Paul - one sent to the Gentiles and the other to the Jews. So, I continue to learn that God is Sovereign and is in control of everything that concerns our lives.

God gave us the ability to make choices. He will not destroy us when we make mistakes, but there will be consequences for our actions. The Bible says, "Remove the edge and the serpent will bite." Therefore, when we step out of God's will by our own choices, the serpent (devil) is waiting to bite – destroy our purpose.

If you realize that you came out from under God's covering, just repent quickly and step back into His place of refuge - the secret place of the Most High God (psalm 91)

There are benefits to isolation. I have produced my best work in isolation. On the day of Pentecost, they were gathered in isolation in adherence to Jesus' command. They received power so great that the whole known world knew that something supernatural had taken place. I am reminded also that when Jesus' time came, leading to His death and resurrection, they were in isolation near the Mount of Olives in the garden of Gethsemane. Jesus was transfigured and was joined by Moses and Elijah, so the disciples got to experience His supernatural   presence.

Moses was also isolated by God a few times. The ones I reflected on most, was the burning bush, and his mountaintop experiences. So awesome was his time with God that people saw the glow from the presence of God upon him. Suffice it to say, amazing things happens when God leads us away in isolation. It is tough but rewarding.

So, the next time you have a sense of being alone, get excited, God has you in isolation because He is getting ready to reveal Himself to you, your family, friends, ministry etc.

JOURNAL

Use this page to write your experiences with God as you go through the chapters of the journey with me.

Chapter 5

Christian's – Fake (counterfeit) or Real (genuine)

This title will become a book, because there is so much in it to be shared. However, I am inserting it in my story because I have encountered so many counterfeit Christians, and I feel the need to bring awareness, regarding this subject, to the Body of Christ.

My experience has been that once a person mention that he/she is a Christian, my tendency was to immediately embrace and accept them into my personal space. I briefly forgot that the word of God says in **Matt. 7:21, "Not everyone who says to me Lord, Lord will enter the Kingdom of heaven, but only the one who does the will of my Father who is in heaven."**

Also, the wheat and the tares must grow together, until the time of harvest.

I was also reminded that everyone, even those in Christ, are somewhat flawed. This is also referred as their dark side. Now, based on my experiences, I realize that some people are raised in families that have extreme dysfunctional background.

Therefore, these dark sides do not necessarily disappear. It can remain with them during their Christian walk. However, as I grew older and more experienced, I learned to operate by this scripture verse, "try the spirit...", in other words, get to know more about a person before you start confiding in them, as it could end up being painful and ultimately detrimental.

Here is a typical example of making the mistake of oversharing without knowing enough about a Christian person. I met someone and immediately became close with the individual because this person is a believer. We started doing ministry activities together and spent quality time in prayer. Many years after, I realized through discernment and Godly wisdom, that the individual lacked integrity and harbored the spirit of gossip and jealousy.

This person would say things that would disrupt unity among members and supporters in my organization. Meanwhile, acting as if all was well between us, when outside of my presence the behavior was undesirable.

The amazing thing about God is that He allowed these experiences to become teachable moments that helped me to avoid similar situations. My God! Did I learn my lessons well!!!

It took a long time for me to walk in this type of wisdom. Let me pause here to say, "These people are not necessarily bad people, they are flawed individuals and if they seek help with their issues, they can be transformed.

I encourage you; submit to the Holy Spirit and the Holy Bible, especially the book of Proverbs. Then make wise decisions regarding knowing who is fake and who is real as Christians. The bible says, "If a man lack wisdom let him ask of God who gives liberally"

The bible also gives a clear understanding of the fruit of the Spirit. So, I encourage you to look for those consistent signs that lack these Godly characteristics. Maya Angelo's quotes, "When someone shows you who they are, believe them the first time."

The scriptures make it very clear how to distinguish the differences. Therefore, there is no excuse. Mistakes can be easily avoided. I facilitated a Bible teaching entitled, "How to develop healthy relationships." Everything that we encounter comes with developmental processes. So, if we want to be wise in our doings, remember that there are signs along the way that will eliminate the problems of mistaking those that are fake for those that are real. There is always a difference if we take time to be observant and discerning.

JOURNAL

Use this page to write your experiences with God as you go through the chapters of the journey with me.

Chapter 6

Making Disciples

Impact Covenant Ministries is an assignment that God gave to me to nurture and contribute to the expansion of His kingdom.

We focus on caring for hurting women and families. This means that, just as Jesus poured His life into the lives of His disciples empowering them to make disciples, so are we mandated to pour out our salvation experience into others.

Let me take you on a little side excursion to

make my point. I have encountered many individuals on my journey, both saved and unsaved. I started doing business in my hometown using my creative gifts, such as sewing, artwork, writing, etc.

There were others around me who were interested in learning how to do some of these creative projects. So, I taught many my skills. However, a mother figure became aware of the fact that I shared my information with others so that they could learn these designer skills. One day she took me aside and said, "Why are you sharing your creative skills with others? They will take it and use it for their benefit." I knew she meant well, however, though we do not have to share the intricacies of our natural creative skills or projects with others, due to its uniqueness. As Christians, God want us to care and share.

So it is, with making disciples, in every sense of the phrase. It is about sharing what we have received from God, allowing others to grow from it, then share what they received with others. The Bible declares, "Every good and perfect gift is from above, coming down from the Father of the heavenly lights, who does not change like shifting shadow."

So, let us not hold back. Instead, let us leave a legacy of our talents, projects, organizations, etc. We should make disciples, so they can continue the work that God allowed us to accomplish. It was meant to be shared. Also, nothing belongs to us. We are stewards and managers. Jesus taught us to make disciples of others.

Proverbs 11:24 taught us that those who scatters will be blessed to the overflow, but those who withholds from others will be like a person with holes in their pockets – everything they put in falls out causing them to end in poverty.

To be at this current level, I had to connect with others who taught me both formally and informally, through training programs and online conferences. Also, informal training by their conduct and example, which were both positive and negative reinforcements. Therefore, even the negative behaviors taught me to be careful how I express myself in the presence of others. We all can influence others - negative or positive.

Sharing the gospel with others require authenticity. Example, Judas' was one of the disciples, but he allowed greed and strong desire for power to seduce him and, ultimately, cost him his life. As I was writing this chapter, it made me think of deceptions I encountered with those who pretended to be Jesus' disciples but lead many new believers astray.

Many started churches built upon merchandising the Gospel. They were also respecters of persons; showing respect to persons who are high on the socioeconomic ladder and very little to those who are of lower estate.

It is very clear why Jesus came out of humble beginnings. God's interest is in training us to reach everyone, regardless of what they look like, sound like, etc. The scripture says, "Go into all the world and preach the gospel to all people"!

When our mindset is renewed on this wise, we will be open to making disciples of all people, not only those who are beneficial to the local church's financial stability. We must reach everyone, regardless of their color, socioeconomic status, etc.

The Bible says, "For God so loved the world, that he gave us His only son, that whosoever believes on Him, shall not perish, but have eternal life." Some believers are guarded, selfish, and harbor prejudices. They only share the Gospel to their culture because it is their comfort zone. But there is a day coming when God will separate the sheep from the goats. There will be consequences. Therefore, let us examine ourselves and cast down anything that will hinder us from completing the work Jesus has started. Reconciling people back to the father.

Please note: We cannot say we are Christians, then disregard and disrespect our brothers or sisters. Disciples are those who follow good examples and training of their teacher.

JOURNAL

Use this page to write your experiences with God as you go through the chapters of the journey with me.

Chapter 7

Going to the Next Level of the Journey

OMG, talking about the grape crushed to get grape juice, or the storms that passes through. I describe this stage of the journey as "tuff" (tough) but fulfilling and rewarding. The only person in the bible, aside from Jesus, who described this kind of experience very well, was Paul.

He said while he and his team were in Asia, they were so pressured, they felt as though they were going to die. Well, that is how I often felt, due to God's processing, as I continued in the work of the Ministry. *2Cor. 1:8, "For we do not want you to be ignorant, brethren, of the affliction we experienced in Asia: for we are so utterly, unbearable crushed that we despaired of life itself."*

So many things happened. It is often said, "It gets worse before it gets better." That was my experience during this process of going to the next level.

These are some of those challenging experiences; There were the circumstances with son. It took everything from us both; brought us to below zero in every aspect of our lives - emotionally, mentally, spiritually, financially... The good thing was these trials allowed me to rely completely on God.

Thankfully, I had great prayer warriors and great friends who stood with us throughout this crisis, but though they were with us, it was still very difficult.

Also, due to my financial crisis, it affected one of my closest friendships; A lack of understanding in the middle of my crisis made everything super challenging. I took responsibility for some of the issues, because, I was trying, with the help of God, to get the matter resolved, but unfortunately it was not resolved on time to stop the sustained damage to our relationship. That was the most heart-wrenching thing I have ever had to bear, and that is all I am going to say about the situation. OMG!

I thank God for His promise, "He will never leave me nor forsake me."

God made a way for me, however, it included having to resume sharing accommodations. He provided the finances to cover my accommodations. The Lord led me to start traveling. So, I decided to seek accommodations with a colleague and was assured that it was ok for a brief period including financial contribution. Upon arrival it was a totally different scenario. I felt worse than I have ever felt anywhere in my life. However, it had to happen, because I believe God wanted me to experience what it feels like to be uncomfortable sharing someone's home.

This helped me to understand and help other traveling Ministers who faced these circumstances. There were many facing these issues during this shift that God made in the life of His Ministers.

However, I did not and will not blame the individual, because all things work together for good to them that love the Lord and are called according to His purpose. But, Oh God, it was tuff(tough). I almost let go, but Jesus kept me, so I would not let go!!!

I also recognized that God had turned up the heat so that I would not get comfortable and remain in one location.

Many years ago, I made a covenant with God and I asked God that when he gives me an assignment out of my comfort zone, and I am apprehensive in going, He has my permission to drag me. He is certainly honoring my request. Be careful what you ask of God.

Another challenge that I faced was being away from my son and new grandson which was very difficult for me, but I remained confident that all things work together for good to them that love God and are called according to His purposes. I also viewed the situation like that of a soldier deployed for duty from his/her family.

I am in full-time Ministry. The moment He called me, He told me to give up my secular job and focus on building the Kingdom organizational assignment He gave to me.

Another challenge was that I encountered many with the spirit of Sanballat, Tobias and Geshem who caused distraction. I tried a few times to reenter the secular employment system, but all doors were shut in my face.

When God shuts a door, no man can open it. I proved that truth.

It is ok for me to develop streams of income, which I did, and continue to do. I cannot seek secular employment. Independent consultant is also in the category of streams of income so that would also be included once He gave permission. I believe, God being the shrewdest in business, knew that to effectively build an organization, it requires complete focus. Luke 16:1-8

He proved this concept in the beginning when He created the Heavens and the earth. All His attention was focused on His design until completed. Then He rested and enjoyed the fruits of His labor. This commitment came with challenges. We, His creation, is certainly not easy to deal with, but He is God - awesome Abba He is. Now I do not care what anyone thinks about my journey in fulltime ministry, even those who I had to borrow from or asked for help, which, thank God were "few and far between".

My Bible tells me, "The earth is the Lords and the fullness thereof..." So, nothing belongs to us. Everything belongs to God. He is the one who gives us the strength to get wealth, hence we would not achieve anything without His strength. I pray that one day we will get that revelation and understanding. I certainly get it. I am not being presumptuous in saying this, but it is truth. Please read the scriptures, it is there.

By extension, I have a friend who is an amazing giver. She says, "I get so excited when Abba allows me the opportunity to give to others." She literally leaps for joy. I am sure she is reminded of the word that says, 'God gives seed to the sower and bread to those who are hungry.' Now, that is someone who know their place in God. She knows that she is a steward of what God gave to her.

Another hardship on the journey upwards, was a time when almost everyone in my organization either had to cut back on their giving or were unable to give consistently to cover the ministry bills and, my God, it was so difficult.

I decided to take on a temporary consulting assignment, which I did sometimes to supplement the ministry's financial shortfall. This assignment came with all the bells and whistles, but the assignment was interrupted midstream, and it had to be placed on hold. I cried out to God and ask how could this be?

This was an amazing opportunity and now it is gone. What am I going to do?

I went to a church the next Sunday and the Minster's sermon was on the story of Peter when he went back fishing after Jesus called him into fulltime ministry. That "stuck" with me as a Rhema Word. It gave me peace amid my financial struggles. You see, He had opened that door temporarily to lead me to a group of hurting women who needed the anointing on my life to destroy the yolks of bondages which was upon their lives. They now testify of God's goodness in sending me their way.

All I will say is God is Sovereign. Though I experienced what looked like setbacks, it was a setup, because after that I got treated like royalty in that region. I have the pictures and videos as proof of what God will do for you when you remain steadfast, unmovable, and abounding in His grace.

God allowed me to be proven by fire as He prepared to elevate/promote me to the next level of ministry. It is often said, "The higher a building is designed to be is the deeper the foundation has to be. The more precious the jewel is, is the more fire it must be processed through. 1Peter 1:7 declares, "These have come so that the proven genuineness of your faith – of greater worth than gold, which perishes even though refined by fire may result in praise, glory and honor when Jesus Christ is revealed." Also, Ecclesiastes 2:5 declares, "For gold is tried in fire, and acceptable men in the furnace of adversity."

Therefore, let me encourage you. Your journey may seem tough and you might feel like giving up, but please do not get weary as you do good in obedience to God, because you will reap, if you do not faint or give up. Believe me, I would not exchange this journey for anything. Tough, but I love it!!

JOURNAL

Use this page to write your experiences with God as you go through the chapters of the journey with me.

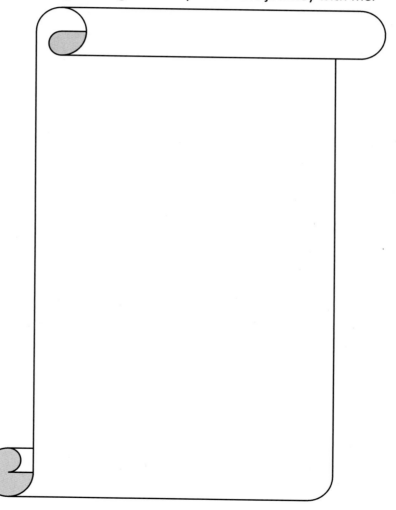

Chapter 8

Traveling for Kingdom Building

My base location for ministry is the State of Florida, USA. I remained in this location for eleven years with very little traveling to other locations. This was God's doing. He told me to treat my ministry as a child going through her developmental stages.

During the formative years of a child, parental attention is critical, especially from ages 0-5 years old. Therefore, I remained obedient to His instructions. At ten years of Ministry, He opened the opportunity to expand the horizon of the ministry. Through our conference line, we were able to reach a nationwide demographics.

I was further instructed to facilitate Intercessory prayer gathering in the Tri-State area. This venture opened the opportunity to meet supporters of our Ministry, who live in the Tri-state area. I knew them only via phone communication. New York was our first stop, then we continued to expand to more states, including Connecticut, Delaware, New Jersey, and Martha's Vineyard in Massachusetts.

Though we facilitated small groups, God allowed an indelible mark to be left upon the hearts of our participants.

At the end of 2016, the Lord directed me to start traveling for ministry and to remain in these areas for three to six months at a time.

To backtrack a bit, the traveling started out as my needing a break to rest from a major challenge God allowed my son and I to go through. This situation took two and a half years to be resolved. It ended in an unexpected way. I then realized that I needed to use wisdom regarding the stress that my body went through. So, I made the decision to go on a break for one month. This took me to the North Eastern States – specifically New Jersey. I got a chance to rest and be restored emotionally, mentally, and physically. It was during this time of rest that the Lord confirmed that I will be traveling for ministry. I was not very clear on what He meant, so I decided to seek His face for clarity.

So, to continue forward, one thing I learned throughout ministry is that when God speaks to us, He is very specific. However, what I experienced is that, many times, we are not focused, centered or in tune with His instructions. Sometimes the cares of the world are so loud in our ears and minds that it drowns out the voice of our God.

The Bible describes His voice as a still small voice. So, I had to find a place of meditation and worship, to clearly hear His voice. There is a song that says, "His voice makes the difference, when He speaks it heals our troubled minds."

As I journeyed through various States, the Lord allowed me to meet one-on-one with women from a diversified list of cultures. There were times when I was hosted in their homes, to walk them through the steps in accomplishing their deliverance. Though some of the space and accommodations were not what I am used to being in, I kept my focus on our Lord and Savior, Jesus Christ.

I remembered there were times when Jesus had no place to lay His head as he spent most of His time among the people who needed deliverance. His disciples learned from His experience and example. So, at times when it got uncomfortable, I would say, "Lord I trust you to see me through to the end."

I have confirmation through the testimonies of those I ministered to. God delivered them from their troubles. Some returned to say thank you, meanwhile others, gratitude failed them, and they were unthankful, but that is all a part of the process.

There were times when they offended me by their behavior, but after a while it became as "water on duck's back." During these times of travel, my ministry base in Florida was disrupted by the enemy and a couple of our Team members moved on. However, again, all things worked together for good.

Through this part of the journey, God confirmed those who was with me and those who were not. I bless them and continue to pray for them. I also will never forget their labor of love to me and to Impact. Again, it is all a part of the process of the journey. If Jesus experience these things, then we will too. He told us to take up our cross and follow him. Also, in this life we will experience problems. But Good News!! Jesus overcame it all, so we must walk in victory.

I can continue to travel and return to base because Impact Covenant Ministries is officially ninety percent virtual. I will pause here for now, and pray that you will be blessed by this second phase of my journey of "My Story, God's Glory"

Stay tuned for the Covid-19 pandemic Journey which hit while I was finishing this edition. Also, my journey of achieving my highest ministerial degree – Ph. D Christian Organizational Leadership.

JOURNAL

Use this page to write your experiences with God as you go through the chapters of the journey with me.

Prescription for Spiritual Wellness

Medications

Vitamin B 66   - The Word of God – Bible

Vitamin P – Prayer (Praying always and in all places)

Vitamin P&W – Praise and Worship (Psalms and Hymns and spiritual songs)

Vitamin BF – Believers Fellowship (Regular Bible Studies and Worship services)

Vitamin SG – Sharing Gospel – Good news (Evangelism/Outreach)

Vitamin R&R – Rest and Recharge/Relaxation (A Time of Retreat)

Directions

Take an unlimited supply of Vitamin B66 daily

Take an unlimited supply of Vitamin P daily

Take two or more doses of Vitamin P&W Daily

Take 2-3 doses of BF weekly

Take daily doses of Vitamin SG

Take 1-2 doses of Vitamin R & R monthly or Bi- annually or as needed.

Maintain this regiment for the remainder of your physical life.

Note the following:

➢ If you fall off the wagon of your regiment, just get right back on.

➢ No need to seek out your primary care (Holy Spirit) because He is always with you guiding you back on the path of spiritual wellness. You just need to clean out your spiritual ears to hear Him.

➢ You cannot overdose on these medications

- This prescription is free. It does not require the affordable care plan or the current to be decided on, T. moronic plan.
- Vitamin B66 was very expensive but now it is free when you download the app
- These vitamins can be taken audibly, visually, by intravenous means or absorption. Whatever type of consumption you take, it will work for you.
- Do your best to stay on course. God bless you!!

Signature: *Father El Elion* - **Author and Finisher of your faith**
Created and published by Rev. Margaret Smith

Traveling to New Jersey

Ministering in Delaware

Ministry from Martha's Vineyard. Visiting a Historical Church

Ministering in New Jersey

Ministering in Connecticut

Ministering in Florida

Ministering from New York

Sep 8

NOTES

NOTES

NOTES

ABOUT THE AUTHOR

Rev. Dr. Margaret Smith achieved her Ph.D. in Christian Organizational Leadership. She is the founder of Impact Covenant Ministries, a women and family resource organization, through which she ministers primarily to hurting women and families as well as meeting the needs of the poor and the mentally challenged.

She is the Author of several books and training manuals. Also produced a DVD and music CD. She is a Licensed and Ordained Minister, who received her theological training from World Outreach Bible School and CCFNI Institutions. She holds a Degree in Christian Counseling and Liberal Arts Studies with concentration in psychology. She is also a trained Fitness and Nutrition Specialist, and is well rounded, having worked in corporate organizations and owned her own business.

Rev. Smith is an anointed speaker/teacher. She ministers in various Christian organizations by teaching the Word of God, conducting conferences, workshops, and open forums throughout the United States.

She has a passion for the youths and has volunteered her services to the Urban League Diversion Summer Camp and in-house programs for five years. She currently facilitates youth training programs, which focuses on self-esteem and self-confidence building.

Rev. Smith has one biological child (son) but many spiritual children whom she feels compelled to pour the Word of God into their lives. She believes that there are no limits in what one can achieve if they put all their trust and confidence in God.

Rev. Smith is available for conferences, workshops, and other speaking engagements www.impactcovenantministries.org. MSMITH@IMPACTCOVENANTMINISTRIES.ORG

NOTES

NOTES

NOTES

NOTES

Made in the USA
Columbia, SC
15 July 2023

20529530R00049